Bible Study Series
for junior high/middle school

THE TRUTH ABOUT Love

Loveland, Colorado

The Truth About Love

Core Belief Bible Study Series

Credits

Editors: Karl Leuthauser and Michael D. Warden
Creative Development Editor: Paul Woods
Chief Creative Officer: Joani Schultz
Copy Editor: Julie Meiklejohn
Art Director: Ray Tollison
Cover Art Director: Jeff A. Storm
Computer Graphic Artist: Eris Klein
Photographer: Jafe Parsons
Production Manager: Gingar Kunkel

ISBN 0-7644-0865-8
10 9 8 7 6 5 4 3 2 1 07 06 05 04 03 02 01 00 99 98

Printed in the United States of America.

Bible Study Series
for junior high/middle school

contents:

the Core Belief: Love

The word "love" in our culture signifies anything from the deepest affections we feel for others to an affinity for chocolate. We need to challenge ourselves to discover the true meaning of the word—an attitude involving action, commitment, and sacrifice. This Core Christian Belief challenges kids to discover this true meaning as it applies to God the Father's love for Christ and the Holy Spirit and to God's self-sacrificing love for people. Studies in this Core Christian Belief also challenge kids to explore how God's love for us should impact our love for him and for others.

the Helpful Stuff

the Studies

Love as a Core Christian Belief

Kids today hear a lot about "love"—from their friends, from movies, and from television. However, what they hear from those sources is often distorted. In the world's terms, love could be a warm feeling of infatuation for another person or an obsession with pizza. This ambiguity can lead people to do all sorts of immoral or hurtful things in the name of "love."

However, the Bible's depiction of love is clear. It speaks of passion, sacrifice, and concern for others. It tells of the fantastic love God has for us—and what that love prompted him to do.

That's why this Core Christian Belief can make a difference in your young people's lives. Developing an accurate, biblical view of love can help your kids understand God better, learn to love him more, and put real love to work in their lives and relationships. When they begin to do those things, they'll truly experience what God and his love are all about.

In the Bible, love means something quite different from what popular culture might tell us. Far more than just a warm feeling of affection, love is also an attitude; it involves action and commitment. It means putting someone else's welfare above your own. Love brings good to the receiver, even though the giver sometimes suffers as a result.

Several different Greek and Hebrew words are translated "love" in the Bible. However, our purpose here isn't so much focused on the various meanings of those terms as it is on the larger concept of love itself.

This course will give kids a good look at exactly what real love looks like, sounds like, and acts like. In the first study, kids will examine the supreme example of **love** in action: Christ's eternal love shown through his death to pay the price for our sins.

Next, kids will explore what love means when responding to a very real issue that touches each of us: **AIDS.** Kids will recognize that the choice to reach out in love to those in need brings with it both a responsibility and an opportunity.

The third study will lead kids to recognize how **trusting others** is one of the cornerstones of real love. In both giving and receiving love, the ability to trust others demonstrates a true commitment and a willingness to risk suffering and pain for the sake of love.

Finally, kids will examine the many things in our world which people use as **substitutes for love.** These can include everything from addictions to drugs or alcohol to the use of pornography. Kids will learn to tell the difference between real love and substitutes, and they'll understand the destructive power of substitutes for love. Love is the quality that shows others we are Jesus' followers. It's what makes friendships, families, and marriages work. It's what prompts people to serve and obey God. And it's what motivates us to share with other people what God has given us and done for us. Love is what makes Christianity a faith of action and not just words.

*For a more comprehensive look at this Core Christian Belief, read Group's **Get Real: Making Core Christian Beliefs Relevant to Teenagers.***

DEPTHFINDER

HOW THE BIBLE DESCRIBES LOVE

To help you effectively guide your kids toward this Core Christian Belief, use these overviews as a launching point for a more in-depth study of love.

- **God the Father's Love for Christ and the Holy Spirit** Though we don't know many details about the inner relationship between the Father, the Spirit, and Jesus Christ, we know it's one of love. God the Father loves Jesus the Son much as a human parent loves his or her own child, and Jesus loves the Father as well. The Holy Spirit provides the bond of oneness and unity between them. That love relationship has existed since before time began; it's part of the nature of God and is demonstrated for us throughout Jesus' life on earth (Matthew 17:5; John 14:31; 17:24; Colossians 1:13; 1 John 4:16).
- **God's Love for Humanity** Though human nature leads people toward loving themselves instead of God, God's nature is to love people. Not many people have the courage to really love someone who totally rejects them. But that's the kind of love God shows for us.

In the Old Testament, God's love is directed primarily at Israel. That love, however, is a personal love, compared to a mother's love for her baby. It's also seen as an eternal love, enduring even human rejection.

In the New Testament, God's love is directed toward the whole world, but more specifically toward individuals than to any group of people. God's love is shown most effectively through the life of Christ. Though he sometimes spoke of the Father's love for us, Christ more often demonstrated God's love by helping and healing people. His ultimate act of love was sacrificing his own life for the sake of the world (Deuteronomy 6:4-5; Isaiah 49:14-15; Mark 1:40-42; John 3:16; Galatians 2:20; Romans 5:6-8).

- **Our Love for God** When God gave the Law at Sinai, he commanded the Israelites to love him. However, our natural tendency is to love ourselves and not God. The Israelites were never able to maintain their love for God for very long. Nevertheless, God is still passionately drawing people to love him. Part of demonstrating our love for God involves loving other people. In fact, the Bible states that if we don't love others, we don't really love God (Deuteronomy 11:1; Matthew 6:24; 22:37; John 14:23-24; 1 John 4:7-21).
- **Our Love for Others** Our love for other people should grow naturally out of our love for God. Jesus encourages us to love one another as he loved us. That love should be directed not only to other Christians, but also to anyone who's in need—including our enemies.

Another part of human love involves the romantic love between a man and a woman. This unique expression of love can be best defined by its desire to forge a lifelong, sacrificial relationship with the other person. Despite this unique quality, husbands and wives must also follow the Bible's guidelines about love between any two people (Genesis 2:24; Song of Solomon 1–8; Matthew 5:43-46; Luke 10:25-37; John 13:35; Galatians 6:10; Ephesians 5:33; 1 Corinthians 13; James 2:8-9, 14-17; 1 John 4:7).

CORE CHRISTIAN BELIEF OVERVIEW

Here are the twenty-four Core Christian Belief categories that form the backbone of Core Belief Bible Study Series:

The Nature of God	Jesus Christ	The Holy Spirit
Humanity	Evil	Suffering
Creation	The Spiritual Realm	The Bible
Salvation	Spiritual Growth	Personal Character
God's Justice	Sin & Forgiveness	The Last Days
Love	The Church	Worship
Authority	Prayer	Family
Service	Relationships	Sharing Faith

Look for Group's Core Belief Bible Study Series books in these other Core Christian Beliefs!

Bible Study Series
for junior high/middle school

Think for a moment about your young people. When your students walk out of your youth program after they graduate from junior high or high school, what do you want them to know? What foundation do you want them to have so they can make wise choices?

You probably want them to know the essentials of the Christian faith. You want them to base everything they do on the foundational truths of Christianity. Are you meeting this goal?

If you have any doubt that your kids will walk into adulthood knowing and living by the tenets of the Christian faith, then you've picked up the right book. All the books in Group's Core Belief Bible Study Series encourage young people to discover the essentials of Christianity and to put those essentials into practice. Let us explain...

What Is Group's Core Belief Bible Study Series?

Group's Core Belief Bible Study Series is a biblically in-depth study series for junior high and senior high teenagers. This Bible study series utilizes four defining commitments to create each study. These "plumb lines" provide structure and continuity for every activity, study, project, and discussion. They are:

- **A Commitment to Biblical Depth**—Core Belief Bible Study Series is founded on the belief that kids not only *can* understand the deeper truths of the Bible but also *want* to understand them. Therefore, the activities and studies in this series strive to explain the "why" behind every truth we explore. That way, kids learn principles, not just rules.
- **A Commitment to Relevance**—Most kids aren't interested in abstract theories or doctrines about the universe. They want to know how to live successfully right now, today, in the heat of problems they can't ignore. Because of this, each study connects a real-life need with biblical principles that speak directly to that need. This study series finally bridges the gap between Bible truths and the real-world issues kids face.
- **A Commitment to Variety**—Today's young people have been raised in a sound bite world. They demand variety. For that reason, no two meetings in this study series are shaped exactly the same.
- **A Commitment to Active and Interactive Learning**—Active learning is learning by doing. Interactive learning simply takes active learning a step further by having kids teach each other what they've learned. It's a process that helps kids internalize and remember their discoveries.

For a more detailed description of these concepts, see the section titled "Why Active and Interactive Learning Works With Teenagers" beginning on page 57.

So how can you accomplish all this in a set of four easy-to-lead Bible studies? By weaving together various "power" elements to produce a fun experience that leaves kids challenged and encouraged.

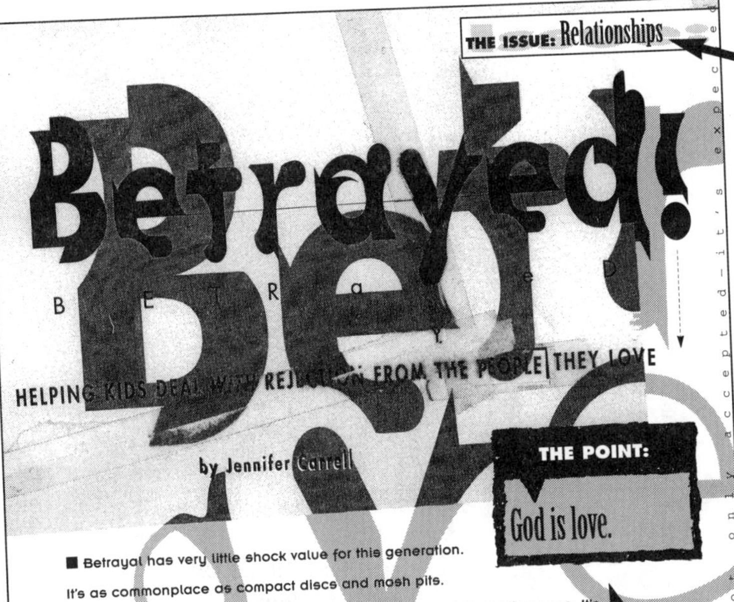

THE ISSUE: Relationships

Betrayed!

HELPING KIDS DEAL WITH REJECTION FROM THE PEOPLE THEY LOVE

by Jennifer Carrell

THE POINT:

God is love.

■ Betrayal has very little shock value for this generation. It's as commonplace as compact discs and mosh pits. For many kids today, betrayal characterizes their parents' wedding vows. It's part of their curriculum at school; it defines the headlines and evening news. Betrayal is not only accepted—it's expected. ■ At the heart of such acceptance lies the belief that nothing is absolute. No vow, no law, no promise can be trusted. Relationships are betrayed at the earliest convenience. Repeatedly, kids see that something called "love" lasts just as long as it's ... permanence. But deep inside, they hunger to see a

- **A Relevant Topic—**More than ever before, kids live in the now. What matters to them and what attracts their hearts is what's happening in their world at this moment. For this reason, every Core Belief Bible Study focuses on a particular hot topic that kids care about.

- **A Core Christian Belief—**Group's Core Belief Bible Study Series organizes the wealth of Christian truth and experience into twenty-four Core Christian Belief categories. These twenty-four headings act as umbrellas for a collection of detailed beliefs that define Christianity and set it apart from the world and every other religion. Each book in this series features one Core Christian Belief with lessons suited for junior high or senior high students.

  "But," you ask, "won't my kids be bored talking about all these spiritual beliefs?" No way! As a youth leader, you know the value of using hot topics to connect with young people. Ultimately teenagers talk about issues because they're searching for meaning in their lives. They want to find the one equation that will make sense of all the confusing events happening around them. Each Core Belief Bible Study answers that need by connecting a hot topic with a powerful Christian principle. Kids walk away from the study with something more solid than just the shifting ebb and flow of their own opinions. They walk away with a deeper understanding of their Christian faith.

- **The Point—**This simple statement is designed to be the intersection between the Core Christian Belief and the hot topic. Everything in the study ultimately focuses on The Point so that kids study it and allow it time to sink into their hearts.

The Study AT A GLANCE

SECTION	MINUTES	WHAT STUDENTS WILL DO	SUPPLIES
Discussion Starter	up to 5	JUMP-START—Identify some of the most common themes in today's movies.	Newsprint, marker
Investigation of Betrayal	12 to 15	REALITY CHECK—Form groups to compare anonymous, real-life stories of betrayal with experiences in their own lives.	"Profiles of Betrayal" handouts (p. 20), highlighter pens, newsprint, marker, tape
	3 to 5	WHO BETRAYED WHOM?—Guess the identities of the people profiled in the handouts.	Paper, tape, pen
Investigation of True Love	15 to 18	SOURCE WORK—Study and discuss God's definition of perfect love.	Bibles, newsprint, marker
	5 to 7	LOVE MESSAGES—Create unique ways to send a "message of love" to the victims of betrayal they've been studying.	Newsprint, markers, tape
Personal Application	10 to 15	SYMBOLIC LOVE—Give a partner a personal symbol of perfect love.	Paper lunch sack, pens, scissors, paper, catalogs

notes:

Betrayed! 16

- **The Study at a Glance—**A quick look at this chart will tell you what kids will do, how long it will take them to do it, and what supplies you'll need to get it done.

THE POINT OF *BETRAYED!*:

God is love.

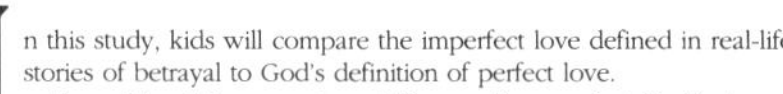

THE BIBLE CONNECTION

1 JOHN 4:7-21 — The Apostle John explains the nature and definition of perfect love.

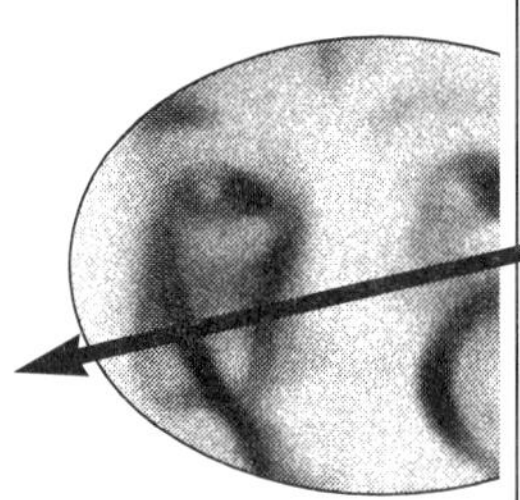

In this study, kids will compare the imperfect love defined in real-life stories of betrayal to God's definition of perfect love.

By making this comparison, kids can discover that God is love and therefore incapable of betraying them. Then they'll be able to recognize the incredible opportunity God of[...] relationship worthy of their absolute trust.

Explore the verses in The Bible Connectio[...] mation in the Depthfinder boxes throughout [...] understanding of how these Scriptures conne[...]

THE STUDY

DISCUSSION STARTER ▼

Jump-Start (up to 5 minutes) As kids arrive, ask them to thin[...] common themes in movies, books, TV show[...] have kids each contribute ideas for a mast[...] two other kids in the room and sharing [...] sider providing copies of People maga[...] what's currently showing on televisio[...] their suggestions, write their respon[...] **come up with a lot of great ide[...] Even tho[...] ent, look through this list an[...] to discov[...] ments most of these themes [...] ave in comm[...]**

After kids make several su[...]gestions, mention[...] responses are connected w[...] the idea of betray[...]

- **Why do you think [...]etrayal is such a co[...]**

Betrayed! 17

LEADER TIP for The Study

Because this topic can be so powerful and relevant to kids' lives, your group members may be tempted to get caught up in issues and lose sight of the deeper biblical principle found in The Point. Help your kids grasp The Point by guiding kids to focus on the biblical investigation and discussing how God's truth connects with reality in their lives.

DEPTHFINDER — UNDERSTANDING INTEGRITY

Your students may not be entirely familiar with the meaning of integrity, especially as it might apply to God's character in the Trinity. Use these definitions (taken from Webster's II New Riverside Dictionary) and other information to help you guide kids toward a better understanding of how God maintains integrity through the three expressions of the Trinity.

Integrity: 1. Firm adherence to a code or standard of values. 2. The state of being unimpaired. 3. The quality or condition of being undivided.

Synonyms for integrity include probity, completeness, wholeness, soundness, and perfection.

Our word "integrity" comes from the Latin word *integritas*, which means soundness. *Integritas* is also the root of the word "integer," which means "whole or complete," as in a "whole" number.

The Hebrew word that's often translated "integrity" (for example, in Psalm 25:21 [NIV]) is *tam*. It means whole, perfect, sincere, and honest.

CREATIVE GOD-EXPLORATION ▼

Top Hats (18 to 20 minutes) Form three groups, with each trio member from the previous activity going to a different group. Give each group Bibles, paper, and pens, and assign each group a different hat God wears: Father, Son, or Holy Spirit. [...] their goal is to write one list describing what God does in the [...]

Holy Profiles

Your assigned Bible passage describes how a particular person or group responded when confronted with God's holiness. Use the information in your passage to help your group discuss the questions below. Then use your flashlights to teach the other two groups what you discover.

- Based on your passage, what does holiness look like?
- What does holiness sound like?
- When people see God's holiness, how does it affect them?
- How is this response to God's holiness like humility?
- Based on your passage, how would you describe humility?
- Why is humility an appropriate human response to God's holiness?
- Based on what you see in your passage, do you think you are a humble person? Why or why not?
- What's one way you could develop humility in your life this week?

- **The Bible Connection**—This is the power base of each study. Whether it's just one verse or several chapters, The Bible Connection provides the vital link between kids' minds and their hearts. The content of each Core Belief Bible Study reflects the belief that the true power of God—the power to expose, heal, and change kids' lives—is contained in his Word.

- **Depthfinder Boxes**—These informative sidelights located throughout each study add insight into a particular passage, word, historical fact, or Christian doctrine. Depthfinder boxes also provide insight into teen culture, adolescent development, current events, and philosophy.

- **Leader Tips**—These handy information boxes coach you through the study, offering helpful suggestions on everything from altering activities for different-sized groups to streamlining discussions to using effective discipline techniques.

- **Handouts**—Most Core Belief Bible Studies include photocopiable handouts to use with your group. Handouts might take the form of a fun game, a lively discussion starter, or a challenging study page for kids to take home—anything to make your study more meaningful and effective.

The Last Word on Core Belief Bible Studies

Soon after you begin to use Group's Core Belief Bible Study Series, you'll see signs of real growth in your group members. Your kids will gain a deeper understanding of the Bible and of their own Christian faith. They'll see more clearly how a relationship with Jesus affects their daily lives. And they'll grow closer to God.

But that's not all. You'll also see kids grow closer to one another.

That's because this series is founded on the principle that Christian faith grows best in the context of relationship. Each study uses a variety of interactive pairs and small groups and always includes discussion questions that promote deeper relationships. The friendships kids will build through this study series will enable them to grow *together* toward a deeper relationship with God.

Kids' DEEPEST Need

How Jesus Fills the Void in Kids' Lives

by Siv M. Ricketts

■ Some of your kids live in poverty. We're not talking about living on the streets and eating from garbage cans. We're talking about an insidious, invisible poverty—the poverty of the heart. These kids live with an emptiness that only one thing can fill. ■ Love. ■ Some of your kids feel loved. Their families and friends actively show how valuable these kids are. But others only know a void deep inside and want so badly to fill it. They hunt for the precious treasure of love, but sometimes the search leads them to treasure chests full of counterfeit money—bad relationships, empty accomplishments, life-threatening addictions. ■ And all the while your kids search, there's a heart that's breaking—the heart of the One who gave his life in exchange for theirs. His love is the true treasure. ■ This study explores the incredible treasure of Jesus' sacrificial love, the only love that can satisfy your kids' deepest need.

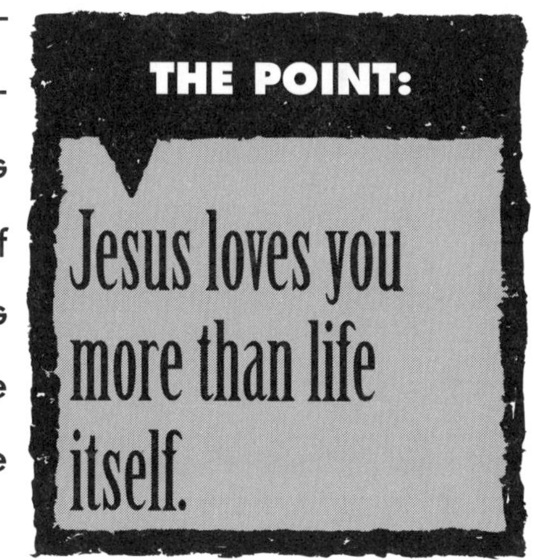

The Study AT A GLANCE

SECTION	MINUTES	WHAT STUDENTS WILL DO	SUPPLIES
Creative Opener	5 to 10	LOOKING FOR LOVE—Look for objects that symbolize where they look for love.	
Bible Exploration	25 to 30	TREASURE HUNT—Create a treasure hunt, and search for verses about Jesus' love.	Bibles, prepared index cards, paper, pencils
Application	15 to 20	SHARE THE TREASURE—Create a campaign to share Jesus' love with others.	Bible, paper, pencils

notes:

THE POINT OF "KIDS' DEEPEST NEED":

Jesus loves you more than life itself.

THE BIBLE CONNECTION

JOHN 3:16; 13:34-35; 15:12-14, 16-17; ROMANS 5:6-8; 8:38-39; and 1 JOHN 4:7-10	These passages describe God's love for us and how we should respond to it by loving one another.
MATTHEW 6:19-21	This passage encourages us to store our treasure in heaven.

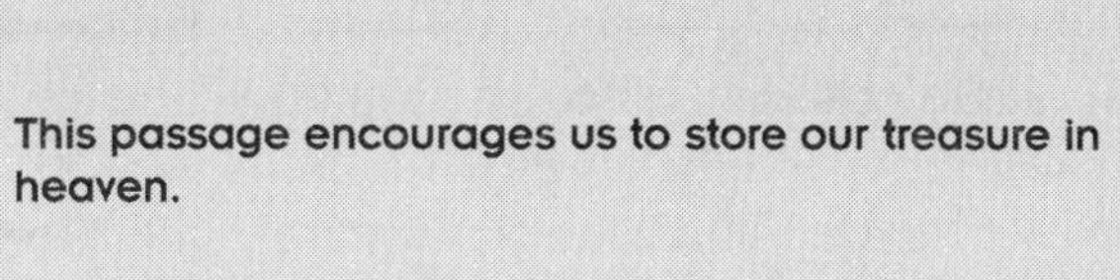

In this study, kids will explore ways they search for love. Then they'll create a treasure hunt and embark upon it, discovering verses about Jesus' love for them along the way.

Through this experience, kids can discover that the only true, fulfilling love is that of Jesus Christ, who loves them more than life itself.

Explore the verses in The Bible Connection, then examine the information in the Depthfinder boxes throughout the study to gain a deeper understanding of how these Scriptures connect with your young people.

BEFORE THE STUDY

Photocopy the sets of Scripture passages and questions from the "No Greater Love" handout" (p. 22). Then cut the sets apart, and paste each to the back of separate index cards. If you have more than twenty students in your class, create two or more cards of each set so you'll have one card for every four students.

for The Study

Because this topic can be so powerful and relevant to kids' lives, your group members may be tempted to get caught up in issues and lose sight of the deeper biblical principles found in The Point. Help your kids grasp The Point by focusing on the biblical investigation and discussing how God's truth connects with reality in their lives.

for The Study

Whenever you tell groups to discuss a list of questions, write the questions on newsprint and tape the newsprint to the wall so each group can answer the questions at its own pace.

THE STUDY

CREATIVE OPENER ▼

Looking for Love

(5 to 10 minutes)

When everyone has arrived, say: **Today we're going to talk about love. To begin, search for something in this room that symbolizes one place where you look for love. For example, you might look for love in sports because people like you when you help your team win. In this example, someone's tennis shoe could symbolize sports. When you find your symbol, don't tell anyone what it is.**

When everyone has chosen a symbol, say: **Now turn to a partner. Within your pairs, each of you must guess what the other person's symbol is. Choose one partner to be the Guesser first. Guessers, look around the room and ask "yes or no" questions to figure out your partner's symbol. When you've guessed the symbol, switch places and let your partner be the Guesser. Ready? Go!**

When the partners have finished, have pairs discuss these questions:

- **How was looking for each other's symbol like looking for love? How was it different?**
- **How did your symbol represent where you look for love?**
- **Where are other places you look for love?**
- **Do you usually find love in those places? Explain.**
- **What makes you feel loved?**
- **How long does that feeling last?**

Invite students to share their responses with the whole class. Then say: **Love is a valuable treasure that we all look for. Today you'll search for and find the most valuable treasure of all—the love of Jesus Christ. <u>Jesus loves you more than life itself.</u>**

BIBLE EXPLORATION ▼

Treasure Hunt

(25 to 30 minutes)

Say: **Love is a treasure we all want to find. As anyone who's hunted treasure can tell you, you can only find treasure when you have an accurate map.**

You're going to create maps that lead to the treasure of Jesus' love. By following the maps you create, you'll discover how <u>Jesus loves you more than life itself.</u>

Have students form groups of no more than four. Give each group a piece of paper, a pencil, and one of the index cards you prepared before the study. Say: **As a group, read your Scripture passage and copy it word for word on the front of your index card. When**

DEPTH FINDER

BLESSING YOUR KIDS

According to Christian therapists Gary Smalley and John Trent in their book *The Blessing*, Orthodox Jews today continue the biblical tradition of blessing their children. In maintaining this tradition, these parents convey love and acceptance and give their children emotional freedom to engage in other intimate relationships.

If your students don't receive blessing from their parents, they'll struggle throughout their adolescence and adulthood, searching for love and self-worth. While you can't ever take their parents' place, you can communicate God's love for them and his acceptance by offering them your blessing. To bless your students, try the following five actions:

1. **Meaningfully touch your students.** Appropriately touch your students to communicate warmth and affirmation.
2. **Speak your message of blessing to your students.** Verbally communicate the blessing to provide genuine acceptance—a lack of negative words is not enough.
3. **Attach high value to your students.** Recognize and affirm your students' gifts, talents, and positive characteristics.
4. **Picture a special future for your students.** Acknowledge that God will use your students in positive ways.
5. **Actively commit to fulfill the blessing in your students' lives.** Commit to doing whatever you can to help your students fully realize their potential.

for Treasure Hunt

If you have enough leaders, you might want to assign one to each group.

you're done, hide your card in a well-lit area near our meeting room, such as a hallway or next to a street light. Then create a treasure map that will lead others from this room to your card. Write the reference of your Scripture passage and all your directions on the piece of paper. For example, you could write "John 3:16. Take ten baby steps straight ahead, turn right, take three steps to the maple tree, turn right, take eight giant steps..." and so on. You may have as many as ten instructions on your map.

You may create instructions that lead others all over the church area, but make sure your map clearly leads from this room to your card. When you've created your map, test it to make sure other groups will be able to find your card. You have ten minutes to hide your card and create your map.

for Treasure Hunt

If it's a rainy day or if you're concerned about your kids disrupting a church service, have groups hide their cards in your meeting room. Or use other church rooms that will be empty—for example, broom closets, vacant classrooms, or hallways.

When everyone has returned to the room, have each group exchange its map with a group that had a different Scripture passage. Say: **You now have ten minutes to follow your new map, find the card, read the verses, and answer the questions. When you're done, present the "treasure" you found—what you learned about Jesus' love for you—to the rest of the group.**

When students have found their treasures and returned to the room, allow groups one minute each to present what they've learned. Then have foursomes discuss these questions:

- **How did you feel when you found your treasure?**
- **How was looking for your treasure like looking for love?**
- **How was it different?**
- **Did you find love on this treasure hunt? Explain.**
- **How is discovering a treasure like discovering someone**

for Treasure Hunt

If you have fifteen or fewer students, have kids form pairs or trios to do this activity. Or have foursomes create maps for more than one card.

for Treasure Hunt

If you have extra time, have kids create one big treasure map, with all groups transferring their directions onto it. Tape several sheets of newsprint together. Mark the location of your meeting room in the middle of the paper. Then have groups write their directions on the giant piece of paper, drawing landmarks and the number of steps needed to get from one landmark to the next. For example, they could draw a tree and a street sign and between the two write "take fifteen steps." Have each group mark an X on the spot where its index card is hidden. Post this giant map outside your meeting room for kids to refer to as they look for the index cards. Have groups look for all of the cards instead of just one. Tell groups that when they find each card, they should read the verses and answer the questions. When they've finished, have groups develop creative presentations of what they learned about God's love through all the Bible passages. Then move to the discussion questions.

DEPTH FINDER — UNDERSTANDING THE BIBLE

In Jesus' time, Jewish men studied under well-known rabbis to become scribes. As a rule, students chose the rabbis they wished to learn from. But Jesus turned the tables. In John 15:16 Jesus said to the disciples, "You did not choose me, but I chose you." He chose the people he wanted to teach.

Jesus still chooses us today. Your kids need to know that Jesus chose to die for them so that they could be with him forever.

loves you? like discovering that Jesus loves you more than his own life?

Have foursomes read Matthew 6:19-21 and discuss these questions:

- **What does this passage say about treasure?**
- **How can you store the treasure of love you find on earth? the love you find in Jesus?**
- **Now that you've found the treasure of Jesus' love, what will you do with it?**

POINT Say: **You've just hunted for Scripture passages to discover that <u>Jesus loves you more than life itself.</u> But Jesus' love isn't hidden from you. Although you may not look for Jesus' love, it's easy to find. You can read God's Word to discover it. You can see how God provides food, clothing, help, and encouragement for you every day. And you can look at a cross to remind yourself of how he sacrificed his life so that you can live forever.**

APPLICATION ▼

Share the Treasure

(15 to 20 minutes)

Have a volunteer read aloud John 13:34-35.

Ask:

- **What does it mean to love others as Jesus loves us?**

POINT After kids have suggested a few answers, say: **You've discovered a wonderful, priceless treasure today—that <u>Jesus loves you more than life itself.</u> The great thing about this treasure is that there's enough for everyone. If you share Jesus' love with others, you'll have more than enough left over for yourself.**

Let's create a Share the Treasure campaign with the goal of allowing Jesus to love others through us. First, let's practice sharing God's love by encouraging and praying for each other.

In their foursomes, have students each say one way the person on his or her left has shared God's love. For example, a student might say, "I saw you show God's love to Alicia when you shared your lunch with her." Then have students each pray that the person on his or her right would experience God's love.

Distribute paper and pencils to the groups. Say: **Now let's brainstorm ideas for our Share the Treasure campaign. In your groups,**

DEPTHFINDER

UNDERSTANDING THE BIBLE

Romans 8:35-39 states that absolutely nothing can separate us from God's love. Even the most evil presence in the spiritual realm cannot keep us from the love God has for us.

Sometimes we choose to disobey God, and our guilt can make us feel as though God has left us. But we're the ones who have created the distance, not God. We can't enjoy Jesus' undying and unconditional love when we sin.

But God promises in 1 John 1:9 that when we confess our sins, he'll forgive us. When we admit our wrongdoing, we're free from guilt and can once again enjoy a loving, healthy relationship with our Father in heaven.

If your students feel far from God's love, encourage them to evaluate whether they've sinned. If they have, remind them that God wants to forgive them and that when they confess they'll be able to experience God's love.

develop one idea for sharing Jesus' love with others. Decide on a target audience, what you'll do to show Jesus' love to those people, and how long you'll run the campaign. For example, you could visit people in convalescent homes and teach them Sunday school lessons once a month for six months. Or you could create "Un-Valentine's Day" cards with verses about Jesus' love to give to your neighbors. Or you could write a Share the Treasure theme song to sing to the congregation during a church service.

You have ten minutes to think of your idea. After ten minutes, each group will present its campaign. Then as a class we'll agree on one idea to carry out.

When groups have brainstormed their campaign ideas, have them present their ideas to the class. Have the whole class vote on a campaign or decide unanimously which one to use. Then make plans to implement the campaign. For example, if the class chooses to create "Un-Valentine's Day Cards" you could have kids volunteer to create artwork, look up verses about God's love, or create poems to copy inside the cards.

POINT

Before kids leave, say: **Jesus loves you more than life itself. As you leave today, remember that this treasure is yours to keep forever. No one can take it away from you. It can't be stolen. It'll never go up in flames. It is always yours. You have the choice to accept or reject what Jesus has already given you.**

As kids leave, allow them opportunities to talk with you about Jesus' love. Some kids may wish to talk to you one-on-one about the new treasure they've discovered and how they can learn more about it.

"No Greater Love"

Photocopy this page, cut these sections apart, and paste each section to the back of separate index cards.

JOHN 3:16—What do you think it was like for God to give his only Son for you? Would you sacrifice someone *you* love for the world? What's your reaction to learning that *Jesus loves you more than life itself?* Now prepare to share with the rest of the class what you've discussed.

JOHN 15:12-14, 16-17—What does this passage say about love? Would you be willing to die for a friend? Why or why not? *Jesus loves you more than life itself*—he died on a cross for you. What's your reaction to that? Now prepare to share with the rest of the class what you've discussed.

ROMANS 5:6-8—Is there anyone in this world you'd die for? If so, who and why? If not, why not? What kind of people did Jesus die for? What's your reaction to learning that *Jesus loves you more than life itself?* Now prepare to share with the rest of the class what you've discussed.

ROMANS 8:38-39—Do you ever feel separated from God? What does this verse say about being separated from God's love? *Jesus loves you more than life itself*—what's your reaction to discovering that nothing can keep you from his love? Now prepare to share with the rest of the class what you've discussed.

1 JOHN 4:7-10—What does this passage say about loving others? What does this passage say about how much God loves you? What's your reaction to learning that *Jesus loves you more than life itself?* How can you show this kind of love to others? Now prepare to share with the rest of the class what you've discussed.

HIV [POSITIVE]

Showing Christian Compassion to Today's "Untouchables"

BY PAMELA J. SHOUP

Showing Christian Compassion to Today's "Untouchables"

■ More than half a million American cases have been reported to Centers for Disease Control and Prevention. ■ At least 18 million people worldwide are infected with it. ■ One quarter of new infections occur among people between the ages of thirteen and twenty-one. ■ It is HIV—the virus that causes AIDS. ■ More than any previous generation, today's young people must face the sobering consequences of immorality run amok. Not only must they protect themselves by avoiding risky behaviors, but they must cope as a generation with a contingent of dying people who need love and compassion. The self-righteous may point fingers and condemn to their fate those infected with HIV or AIDS. But AIDS is a disease, not a crime—its victims need mercy, not judgment. ■ This study invites kids to actively show love to today's growing population of "untouchables"—victims of HIV and AIDS.

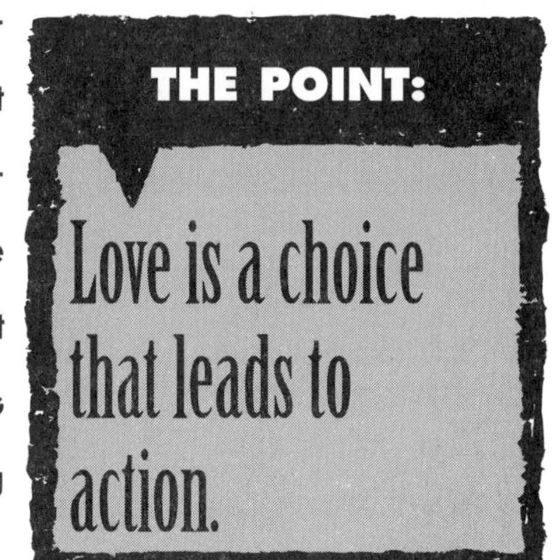

The Study AT A GLANCE

SECTION	MINUTES	WHAT STUDENTS WILL DO	SUPPLIES
Creative Opener	15 to 20	A PERFECT WORLD—Create pictures of their "perfect worlds," and explore how "imperfect" people fit into their worlds.	Bibles, newsprint, tape, colored markers
Bible Exploration	10 to 15	A CIRCLE OF FRIENDS—Experience being "outside the circle" as one with HIV/AIDS might feel.	Bibles, slips of paper, pen
Relational Exploration	15 to 20	IT CAN'T HAPPEN TO ME—Brainstorm and role play ways to reach out to people with HIV/AIDS.	Bibles, "It Can't Happen to Me" handout (p. 31), self-stick notes, pencils
Closing	up to 5	LOVE IN ACTION—Design a card for a local HIV/AIDS support group or agency.	Poster board, colored markers

notes:

THE POINT OF "HIV POSITIVE":

Love is a choice that leads to action.

THE BIBLE CONNECTION

MATTHEW 25:31-46	Jesus promises a place in his kingdom for those who help the sick.
LUKE 5:12-14	Luke relates how Jesus touched and healed a man suffering from a contagious skin disease.
1 JOHN 4:19-21	John explains that those who love God must also love others.

In this study, kids will create pictures of their "perfect worlds" and study Scripture passages to discover where HIV and AIDS victims fit into their worlds.

Through this experience, kids can discover their responsibility to show love and compassion to people who have HIV or AIDS.

Explore the verses in The Bible Connection, then study the information in the Depthfinder boxes throughout the study to gain a deeper understanding of how these Scriptures connect with your young people.

LEADER TIP for The Study

Because this topic can be so powerful and relevant to kids' lives, your group members may be tempted to get caught up in issues and lose sight of the deeper biblical principles found in The Point. Help your kids grasp The Point by focusing on the biblical investigation and discussing how God's truth connects with reality in their lives.

BEFORE THE STUDY

Gather newsprint, tape, and colored markers. Tape a sheet of newsprint to a wall for each group of three or four students.

For the "Circle of Friends" activity, cut enough slips of paper for each student to have one. On about one-fourth of the slips, write "HIV positive." On the others write "healthy."

Photocopy the quotations from the "It Can't Happen to Me" handout (p. 31), and cut them apart. If you have more than ten students in your class, you'll need to photocopy the handout more than once. You might also want to photocopy the "The Facts About HIV and AIDS" Depthfinder (p. 29) for each student.

THE STUDY

CREATIVE OPENER ▼

for A Perfect World

If you wish, provide objects such as paper clips, paper cups or plates, stickers, or any other items kids can use to create pictures.

A Perfect World

(15 to 20 minutes)

When everyone has arrived, have kids form groups of three or four. Set out colored markers and a sheet of newsprint for each group. Say: **Pretend that we live in a perfect world. No one hurts; there's no crime; everyone's happy. With your group, use a sheet of newsprint and the other items I've provided to create a picture of your perfect world.**

After five minutes, let each group briefly describe its perfect world to the whole group. Say: **Now draw or write on your pictures how the following groups of people would affect your perfect world: people who are mentally or physically handicapped, people who are starving, orphans, and the elderly. For example, would they change the look on people's faces, the color of the sky, or the sounds you might hear in your world?**

When groups have revised their perfect worlds, have them explain their "new" pictures to the class. Then have groups read 1 John 4:19-21 and discuss these questions:

- **Based on 1 John 4:19-21, how does God want us to treat people who go through difficult circumstances?**
- **Having read these verses, do you want to revise your picture again? Explain.**

Allow kids to revise their pictures if they wish and explain their changes.

POINT Say: **God wants us to show our love for him by loving others. <u>Love is a choice that leads to action,</u> and today we'll focus on ways to show Christ's love to people with HIV and AIDS.**

LEADER TIP

for The Study

The Centers for Disease Control and Prevention have a hot line available for questions or statistics about HIV/AIDS. If your kids have questions you can't answer, have them call the hot line at 800-342-2437.

BIBLE EXPLORATION ▼

A Circle of Friends

(10 to 15 minutes)

Have kids stand in a circle, and hand each student one of the slips of papers you prepared before the study. Tell kids not to show anyone what's written on their slips of paper yet.

Say: **If you have a slip of paper that says "HIV positive," think about how you would feel if you really were HIV positive. If your paper says "healthy," think about what it means to not have an HIV-positive note. Now choose a partner near you, and quietly share the contents of your paper with him or her.**

Allow kids a few seconds to share their notes with their partners and then have pairs follow these instructions (allow kids ten to fifteen

DEPTHFINDER UNDERSTANDING THE BIBLE

Approximately 80 to 85 percent of AIDS cases in the United States are associated with homosexual activity, bisexual activity, and IV drug usage. About 75 percent of AIDS cases in the world are the result of heterosexual transmission.

God clearly condemns most behaviors through which people contract HIV/AIDS. The Bible denounces the homosexual lifestyle in Leviticus 18:22; 20:13; and Romans 1:24-27. The Bible warns against drug abuse in passages such as 1 Peter 4:1-6. In 1 Corinthians 6:9-11 and 1 Timothy 1:8-11 God commands us to avoid any sexual behavior outside of marriage.

With these passages in their arsenals, Christians often point their fingers at HIV and AIDS sufferers. The fact that someone has contracted HIV or AIDS "clearly communicates" his or her sinful nature. Many Christians, sadly, believe that HIV/AIDS victims deserve their fate.

But "all have sinned and fall short of the glory of God" (Romans 3:23). We *all* need God's mercy—no one is more guilty than another. And God has offered his forgiveness to *all* who've disobeyed him (see Acts 10:43; Ephesians 1:7; and 1 John 1:9). The Christian community needs to communicate God's mercy by showing compassion to victims of HIV/AIDS regardless of the ways these victims have contracted the disease.

Use the information in this Depthfinder to help kids understand God's view of the behaviors leading to AIDS and God's gift of forgiveness for those behaviors.

for The Study

Whenever you tell groups to discuss a list of questions, write the questions on newsprint and tape the newsprint to the wall so each group can discuss the questions at its own pace.

seconds between instructions):

- **Tell your partner a secret.**
- **Tell your partner something you like about him or her.**
- **Give your partner a hug.**

Gather kids back into a circle, and have the people with HIV-positive slips sit in the center of the circle. Ask:

- **For those of you in the center of the circle, how did it feel to get an HIV-positive note? to interact with your partner? to have to sit in the center of the circle?**
- **For those of you in the outer circle, what did you think when your partners had HIV-positive notes? How did you treat your "HIV-positive" partners? How did it feel to touch someone who was "HIV positive"?**
- **If neither you nor your partner had an HIV-positive note, how did that make you feel?**

Have kids form one circle and pass their slips of paper slowly around the circle so everyone holds an HIV-positive paper at least once. As students pass their slips of paper, say: **When one of our friends has HIV or AIDS, we're all touched by the disease. It affects our lives as we learn how to love that friend through a difficult, painful time.**

Have students return to their pairs, read Matthew 25:31-46, and discuss these questions:

- **What does God promise for those who help the sick? for those who refuse to help?**
- **Based on this Scripture passage, how will you treat AIDS**

sufferers in the future?

Say: **The Scripture passage we just read illustrates that <u>love is a choice that leads to action.</u> We must help those who are sick. To be better equipped to help HIV and AIDS sufferers, let's explore how it might feel to have these illnesses.**

RELATIONAL EXPLORATION ▼

for It Can't Happen to Me

If kids don't know HIV/AIDS victims personally, encourage them to do something kind for a local AIDS agency or support group or for someone in a nearby hospital.

It Can't Happen to Me (15 to 20 minutes)

Using the information in the "The Facts About HIV and AIDS" Depthfinder (p. 29), explain some of the facts about the diseases to the group. Then ask:

- **Do you think you could ever get AIDS? Why or why not? What kinds of choices can you make to avoid HIV/AIDS?**
- **How does knowing how you can and can't contract HIV affect the way you'll relate to those who have HIV or AIDS?**

Say: **<u>Love is a choice that leads to action.</u> You can love yourself by choosing to avoid most of the behaviors that expose you to AIDS. You can love those with AIDS by touching them with your own life.**

Have kids form pairs (or return to their pairs from the "Circle of Friends" activity). Instruct pairs to read Luke 5:12-14 and then discuss these questions:

- **How is Jesus' touching the leper like the way you treat people with AIDS? How is it different?**
- **How might you "touch" people who have HIV/AIDS?**

While pairs discuss these questions, give each pair a quote from the "It Can't Happen to Me" handout (p. 31), some self-stick notes, and a pencil. If you have more than ten students, give the same quote to two or more groups.

Say: **We can show love to HIV and AIDS sufferers in many ways. Read the quote I've given you and then discuss ways you could help this person. Designate one partner as the "victim" and one as the friend. As you brainstorm ways to show love to HIV/AIDS victims, write each action on a self-stick note and stick the note to the victim. Then choose one of the actions you've written and create a role-play showing how you'd touch this friend's life. Start your role-play by having the victim read the quote I gave you.**

If kids need help brainstorming loving actions, here's a list of ideas to help: Visit HIV/AIDS victims often; touch and hug them; weep and laugh with them; offer to help with chores or feeding of pets; bring food, books, magazines, or posters; bring along another friend; go for a walk or outing; help celebrate the holidays; send a card that says, "I care"; listen to them; read to them; talk with them about the future; listen to music or watch TV; pray together; take them to church; and bring a positive attitude.

Let pairs meet for five minutes to brainstorm their ideas and create their role-plays. Then gather everyone back together and allow

DEPTHFINDER

THE FACTS ABOUT HIV AND AIDS

What are HIV and AIDS? How are they related? And how can I avoid getting them? These are the questions your students may ask about HIV/AIDS. They need answers if they're to protect themselves and freely show love to HIV and AIDS sufferers.

Following are some answers to the most compelling questions about HIV and AIDS. Consider photocopying this Depthfinder as a reference for your kids.

- **What do the terms "HIV" and "AIDS" mean?** "HIV" stands for Human Immunodeficiency Virus. This virus causes AIDS—Acquired Immunodeficiency Syndrome.
- **What happens to someone who contracts HIV/AIDS?** HIV breaks down a person's immune system—the infected person loses the ability to protect himself or herself from germs that most of us can fight. These germs cause cancers, pneumonia, and other infections that lead to death, usually within ten years after HIV is diagnosed. When an HIV-positive person contracts one of these diseases, he or she is considered to have AIDS. At this time, there is no vaccine or cure for HIV or AIDS.
- **How does someone get HIV/AIDS?** HIV is spread through vaginal, anal, or oral sex with someone who is infected with HIV; sharing needles for injecting drugs; or in childbirth or breast-feeding, passed from an infected mother to her child. You can no longer contract HIV/AIDS through blood transfusions—since 1985, all donated blood has been tested for HIV, and today's blood supply is considered safe.

You **cannot** get AIDS from hugs; handshakes; coughs or sneezes; sweat or tears; pets; mosquitoes or other insects; eating food prepared by someone else; or using toilet or shower facilities, eating utensils, drinking fountains, sports equipment, or swimming pools.

- **Who is most likely to get HIV/AIDS?** HIV/AIDS is a disease that does not discriminate. It doesn't matter whether you are male or female, gay or straight or bisexual, old or young. Anyone can get it. But you can keep from contracting the disease if you avoid risky behaviors.
- **What specifically can I do to avoid contracting this disease?** You should
  - be sexually abstinent until marriage;
  - avoid drugs;
  - not drink, since drinking often leads to risky behavior; and
  - become educated about HIV/AIDS.

Keep in mind that scientists learn more about this disease all the time. The information included in this Depthfinder is the most accurate information we have at the time of printing. Continue to educate yourself about this disease by researching new developments as they arise.

(Information compiled from American Red Cross brochures "HIV and AIDS" and "Teenagers and HIV" and the Centers for Disease Control and Prevention.)

pairs to present their role-plays and read the ideas stuck to their victims.

Then have pairs discuss these questions:

- **What's your reaction to the quotes we read? to the ways people chose to "touch" HIV and AIDS victims?**
- **What's your reaction to being a victim in this activity? How**

If you have any artists in your group, invite them to decorate the card as well. You might supply glitter, stickers, glue, construction paper, and tape as decorating materials.

did it feel to be "touched" by the ideas your partner stuck to you?

- **What's your reaction to being a helper? How did it feel to touch your partner?**
- **How will this experience affect how you'll treat HIV or AIDS sufferers in the future?**

Say: **<u>Love is a choice that leads to action.</u> Let's commit to putting one of our ideas into action this week. Have students share with their partners ways they'll show love to HIV/AIDS victims this week.**

Then have pairs pray aloud or silently for people suffering from HIV/AIDS. Students could pray for healing, for endurance during a difficult time, or for a way to help someone who has the virus.

Say: **Now let's put our love into action and create a prayer card for people in our area who have HIV or AIDS.**

CLOSING ▼

If logistically possible, close your meeting by delivering the card as a group.

Love in Action (up to 5 minutes)

Have kids brainstorm a message to communicate to HIV/AIDS victims, such as "Jesus loves you, and we do, too!" When the group has agreed on a saying, fold a sheet of poster board in half like a card and use a marker to write the saying in big letters on the outside of the card.

Provide colored markers, and invite each student to write a message on the card. Students could write encouraging Bible verses or messages such as "We care" or "I'll pray for you every day." Sign the name of your church and youth group or class and designate students to deliver the card to a local AIDS support group or agency in your city or county.

"If anyone says,

yet hates his brother, he is a liar. For anyone who does not love his brother, whom he has seen, cannot love God, whom he has not seen."

—1 John 4:20

"When I first found out Ben was HIV positive, I was suddenly afraid...I realized I had so many fears about AIDS and did not know much about it. I wanted to be supportive, but I didn't want to do or say the wrong thing...Once I knew the facts, I came to realize that my fears were unfounded. I learned that what Ben needed was my love and support. He needed my hugs, tears, and laughter. What he needed was for me to treat him like a friend."

– ("Colorado Responds to HIV/AIDS," brochure by the AIDS Coalition for Education)

"I'm in a nightmare...I can see Dr. Talbert's face with his eyes all glazed up...then he slowly tells me that my blood samples have come back, and I have...the HIV virus! His mouth keeps moving, but I can't hear words anymore. I can't feel; I can't think. I may be dumb and young and naive, but I'm not stupid. Someone's made the most horrible of horrible mistakes. How could I have...AIDS?...From far off in the distance, I could hear myself sobbing, frightened, little-girl, almost-baby sobs. They wouldn't stop. They will never stop!"

– (*It Happened to Nancy: A True Story From Her Diary* by an anonymous teenager, edited by Beatrice Sparks)

"There is nothing in this world that is worth your life being compromised for. Nothing. No guy, no girl, no matter how cute they may be, is worth waking up to this every day."

– Kerry, age 18, HIV positive (*Just Like Us: AIDS Prevention*, video by Sunburst Communications)

"I wish I didn't have HIV. It is really important to me that I would be able to tell people about my condition and have them understand what it would be like."

– Andy Tuff, 14, a hemophiliac who died of AIDS (Denver Post)

"He always said that if he told a person he had cancer, the person would probably hug him; if he told them AIDS, they'd be scared and walk away."

– Alex Escarano in an article about Pedro Zamora of MTV's Real World. Zamora died of AIDS at age 22 on November 11, 1994. (People magazine)

Trust No One!

Combating the First Rule of Survival In Today's Teenage World

by Matt Dirks

■ Your junior-highers have grown up in a world that discourages trust. Their ability to trust has been diminished—by authority figures who betray them, family members who flake out on commitments, or friends who desert them when times are tough. Their experiences have taught them that trust can be painful—including trust in God. ■ If trust is a vital part of love, as Paul affirms in 1 Corinthians 13, your kids cannot fully obey the Great Commandment to love God and love their neighbors until they learn to trust. Far from blind faith in the world, the trust that God desires is built on wise, yet unconditional love toward others. It's a love that may not be appreciated or returned, but it forms the foundation of obedience to Christ. ■ Nothing in our world can be fully trusted. But junior-highers need to see that the benefits of loving and trusting others far outweigh the costs. They need to understand that it's up to them to end the cycle of mistrust by committing to be trustworthy themselves.

The Study AT A GLANCE

SECTION	MINUTES	WHAT STUDENTS WILL DO	SUPPLIES
Opening Experience	15 to 20	BLIND TRUST—Complete a wheelbarrow race through an obstacle course with one person blindfolded and then discuss the experience.	Chairs, tables, blindfolds, treats for everyone
Bible Connection	25 to 30	TALES OF TRUST—Read Bible stories and then create and perform skits based on their stories. Discuss why each Bible character chose to trust and what resulted from his or her trust.	Bibles, paper, pens
Reflection and Commitment	10 to 15	WHO, WHEN, AND HOW MUCH TO TRUST—Discuss why they choose to trust or distrust others, and discover qualities that make a person trustworthy. Commit to work on the ability to trust others and on their own trustworthiness.	Bible, "Who's to Trust?" handouts (p. 41), pens, newsprint, large marker, tape, "Love Always Trusts" Depthfinder (p. 38)

notes:

THE POINT OF "TRUST NO ONE!":

Real love requires trust.

THE BIBLE CONNECTION

GENESIS 22:1-19	God commands Abraham to sacrifice his son Isaac. Abraham trusts God and intends to obey, while Isaac trusts his father to do God's will.
JUDGES 16:4-21	Blinded by his desires, Samson is fooled into trusting Delilah.
RUTH 1:1-18	Widowed by her husband, Ruth decides to trust her mother-in-law Naomi and follow her.
1 CORINTHIANS 13:6-7	Paul explains that true love carries with it unfailing trust and optimism in our relationships with others.

In this study, students will participate in a trust-building team race, examine trust through the eyes of several Bible personalities, and determine what qualities make a person trustworthy.

Through these experiences, kids can discover what it feels like to be completely dependent on another person and commit to taking practical steps toward trusting others and becoming trustworthy themselves.

Explore the verses in the Bible Connection, then examine the information in the Depthfinder boxes throughout the study to gain a deeper understanding of how these Scriptures connect with your young people.

BEFORE THE STUDY

For the "Blind Trust" activity, set up a challenging obstacle course using chairs and tables. Create a maze that has only one way out by placing the chairs in zigzagging lines. Make the path about three feet wide and then form tunnels by setting up tables across the path. Also, construct bridges in the path by placing two chairs together with their seats facing each other.

For the "Who, When, and How Much to Trust" activity, write the following quote from William Barclay's Daily Study Bible Series: *The Letters to the Corinthians* on newsprint and tape the newsprint to the wall: "We make people what we believe them to be. If we show that we do not trust people, we may make them untrustworthy. If we show people that we trust them absolutely, we may make them trustworthy."

for The Study

Because this topic can be so powerful and relevant to kids' lives, your group members may be tempted to get caught up in issues and lose sight of the deeper biblical principle found in The Point. Help your kids grasp The Point by guiding them to focus on the biblical investigation and discussing how God's truth connects with reality in their lives.

THE STUDY

OPENING EXPERIENCE ▼

Blind Trust

(15 to 20 minutes)

Gather kids at one end of the obstacle course you made before the study. Form teams of two, and give each team a blindfold. Say: **You're going to take a "wheelbarrow" trek through this obstacle course. One person on each team is the wheelbarrow. You must go through the course walking on your hands while your partner holds up your legs. The person who is pushing the wheelbarrow must wear a blindfold. The person who is the wheelbarrow must guide his or her partner through the obstacle course, giving instructions to him or her about when to turn, duck, or step up. If the wheelbarrow's legs touch the floor (except in the tunnels), the team must go back to the start and begin again.**

Have pairs get ready at the starting line and then say: Go! Watch for wheelbarrows whose legs touch the ground. After all the teams have crossed the finish line, offer them a round of applause, and award everyone a treat, such as fruit, candy, gum, or soft drinks.

After the race, have partners discuss these questions:

- **Was it easy or hard for you to trust your partner? Explain.**
- **Did your partner fail you at times in the race? If so, why did you keep on going in the race?**
- **How is this race like trusting people in real life?**
- **In life, is it easy or hard for you to trust other people? Explain.**
- **Why does it feel safer sometimes to not trust anyone?**
- **When someone you trust disappoints you, is it easy or hard for you to trust that person again? Explain.**

After the discussion, have pairs share some of their insights with the whole group. Then say: **Real love requires trust, but trusting other people is hard these days, especially when someone we trust lets us down. Nevertheless, trust is required in the kind of loving relationships God wants us to have with each other. Let's find out why God thinks trust is so important.**

for Blind Trust

Station a few volunteers or older students at regular intervals in the obstacle course to assist the teams as "Safety Techs." Instruct them to watch carefully to prevent students from falling over or being trampled in the mad dash.

If you're concerned that someone may get hurt in the race, consider having pairs take turns racing against the clock instead of having everyone start at the same time.

for Blind Trust

If a wheelbarrow race won't work with your students (because some are in dresses or some may not be strong enough), have them navigate the obstacle course in a piggyback race—place the blindfold on the student giving the piggyback ride and have the "rider" direct him or her through the course. Or, if you prefer, simply blindfold one person and have his or her partner stand on the side and give verbal commands to direct the blindfolded partner to the finish line.

BIBLE CONNECTION ▼

Tales of Trust

(25 to 30 minutes)

Form three teams. Assign one of the following passages of Scripture to each group:

- Genesis 22:1-19

DEPTHFINDER
UNDERSTANDING SAMSON'S DILEMMA WITH DELILAH

Many people misunderstand this passage from Judges 16:4-21. Samson's power wasn't dependent on the length of his hair but on what it symbolized: his commitment to God. Samson's relationship with Delilah was the rock-bottom result of a long downward slide in his relationship with the Lord. Long before he was physically blinded by the Philistines, Samson was spiritually blinded by his greed and lust. His trust in Delilah, who repeatedly proved herself untrustworthy, was made possible because Samson was so deluded by his desires.

We, too, can be blindly led by our desires to trust someone we shouldn't. The desire for physical beauty can lead us to trust the late-night-TV salesman pitching the latest diet craze. The desire for love and acceptance can lead us to trust the first person who shows an interest in us. Before we trust someone, we must learn to check our motives: Are we trusting out of genuine love or because we want something from that person that will make us feel better about ourselves?

- Judges 16:4-21
- Ruth 1:1-18

Have members of each team read their assigned passage together out loud (one or two verses per student) and then instruct team members to create a short skit with simple lines that will tell the story they just read. Tell them that they must create a unique role in their skit for every member of the team. If they run out of human characters, teams can cast players in roles such as animals, trees, or even the wind. Give each team a pen and a sheet of paper.

Say: **Before you start, there's one more thing: Each skit must have one change in the story from the way the Bible tells it. It can be a big change or a small change. After each group presents its skit, each of the other two groups will try to guess which part of the skit we can't trust.**

Give the teams about ten minutes to prepare and then have the first team perform its skit from Genesis. After the first team is finished, have the class give a round of applause. Then say: **Now the other two teams have thirty seconds to decide which part of the skit can't be trusted.** After thirty seconds have passed, ask each team for its answer. Then ask the performing team to give the correct answer.

Have the entire group discuss these questions:

- **What made Isaac trust his father Abraham?**
- **What benefits did trust bring?**
- **What risks were involved?**
- **What were the consequences of Isaac's trust in Abraham?**
- **If you were in Isaac's shoes, would you have trusted Abraham? Why or why not?**

Have the next team perform the skit from Judges. After the team finishes, give the other teams thirty seconds to decide which part of the skit couldn't be trusted and then have the performing team give the correct answer. Ask:

- **What made Samson trust Delilah?**
- **What benefits did trust bring?**

for Blind Trust

It may be difficult for your group to switch gears from the highly physical race to the discussion that follows. If you anticipate such a problem, try moving to a different room or area for the remainder of the study. It's amazing how a change of environment can affect a student's concentration level.

If no other room is available, smooth the transition by giving each team a large piece of aluminum foil and giving teams one minute to create their own trophies to commemorate their participation in the race.

for Tales of Trust

If you have more than twenty kids in your group, form six teams instead of three for this activity and assign each Scripture passage twice.

for Tales of Trust

At first, your students may be inclined to give "churchy" responses to the discussion questions regarding the stories from the Bible. "If I were Samson," they might say, "I would have never trusted Delilah!" Encourage them to dig a little deeper and put themselves in the shoes of these Bible characters. What were the real motivations behind the actions they took? What was going on in their heads (and hearts) as they put their lives in other people's hands?

DEPTH FINDER

LOVE ALWAYS TRUSTS

The kind of love Paul talks about in 1 Corinthians 13 assumes the best in every person—not only when there is reason to trust, but even when trust has been broken. Love stretches faith and "covers the faults of others rather than delighting in them" *(The Expositor's Bible Commentary, Volume 10)*.

However, while love believes the best of all people, it does not rule out common sense. As Proverbs 14:15 puts it, "A simple man believes anything, but a prudent man gives thought to his steps." As we strive to be unconditional in our love toward others, this does not mean extending unconditional trust. Assuming the best in other people does not include placing those things that are most valuable to us blindly into their hands. Trust and wisdom should be inseparable in our relationships with others.

To look at the issue of love and trust in more depth, take a look at these verses:

- Psalm 118:8-9
- Jeremiah 17:5-7
- Matthew 5:43-45
- 1 John 4:18-21

- **What risks were involved?**
- **What were the consequences of Samson's trust in Delilah?**
- **If you were in Samson's shoes, would you have trusted Delilah? Why or why not?**

Have the next team perform the skit from Ruth. Then give the other teams thirty seconds to decide which part couldn't be trusted. After thirty seconds, have the performing team give the correct answer. Ask:

- **What made Ruth trust Naomi?**
- **What benefits did trust bring?**
- **What risks were involved?**
- **What were the consequences of Ruth's trust in Naomi?**
- **If you were in Ruth's shoes, would you have trusted Naomi? Why or why not?**

After all the teams have presented their skits, gather everyone together and ask:

- **How was trying to find the "lie" in each skit like the way we question people's actions or motives in real life?**
- **Should we automatically trust everyone we meet? Why or why not?**
- **How do you build trust in relationships?**
- **What do you do when trust is broken?**
- POINT **In your close relationships, does real love require trust? Why or why not?**
- POINT **If real love requires trust, how loving do you think you are?**
- **How loving are you compared to the Bible characters we just portrayed?**

for The Study

Whenever groups discuss a list of questions, write the questions on newsprint and tape the newsprint to the wall so groups can discuss the questions at their own pace.

Say: <u>Real love requires trust.</u> **But trust comes more easily with some people than with others. Let's take a moment to think about who we really trust in life.**

REFLECTION AND COMMITMENT ▼

Who, When, and How Much to Trust

(10 to 15 minutes)

Have students rejoin the pairs they formed in the "Blind Trust" activity. Give each student a copy of the "Who's to Trust?" handout (p. 41) and a pen. Say: **Think silently of one person you really trust. It could be one of your parents. It could be a teacher, a good friend, or just about anyone else.**

Give students a few moments to think quietly. Then say: **On the left side of your handout, write some of the reasons you trust this person. For example, it could be because he or she is always available for you or because he or she makes wise decisions.** When kids are finished, have them share their ideas with their partners.

Say: **Now think silently of one person who you do not trust. Without mentioning any names, write on your handout the reasons you distrust this person. Maybe it's because he or she gossiped about you or because he or she never follows through on commitments. When you're done, share your ideas with your partner.**

While kids are sharing, tape a sheet of newsprint to the wall. Label one side "I trust people when they..." Label the other side "I distrust people when they..."

When pairs are finished, ask kids to share some of the reasons they have for trusting or distrusting people. Use a marker to write their responses on the newsprint

Say: **The two most important commandments that God gives us in the Bible are in Matthew 22:37-40, where Jesus commands us to love the Lord our God with all our heart, soul and mind, and love our neighbor as ourselves. Our whole relationship with God rests on how well we obey these commandments. And the Bible tells us that one of the most important parts of loving God and loving other people is trusting them. Here's what Paul says about love in 1 Corinthians 13.**

Read aloud **1 Corinthians 13:6-7.**

Say: **The Bible tells us that** <u>**real love requires trust.**</u> **But that's a pretty extreme thing to ask of us. Think about the person you described on the right side of your handout.**

Ask:

- **How much do you think God wants you to trust that person?**
- **Is there a limit to your trust? Why or why not?**
- **Based on what we've learned so far, at what point in a relationship should we stop trusting someone?**

Form groups of four, and give each group a copy of the "Love Always Trusts" Depthfinder (p. 38). Have members of each group read the Depthfinder together and then tell whether they agree, disagree, or partly agree with what the Depthfinder says. Ask kids to explain their answers.

After groups have had time to discuss, get everyone's attention and ask:

- **So, what's the dividing line between unconditional love and trust and common sense?**

Direct kids' attention to the quote you wrote on newsprint before the study. Then ask:

- **Do you agree with this statement? Why or why not?**

POINT

Say: **Deciding when to trust can be hard. But there's one thing we know—real love requires trust. If we want to love the way Jesus loved, we have to extend trust to others and be worthy of their trust as well.**

Think for a moment about one practical step you could take to be more trusting. It could be with one particular person, or it could be with others in general. Write it on your handout and then share it with your group.

When kids are finished, say: **Now think for a moment about one practical step you could take to be more trustworthy—to make others want to trust you. It could be with your parents, with your teachers, or maybe with your friends. Write it on the handout and then share it with your group.**

After groups have shared, have each student tell the other members of his or her group one characteristic he or she sees in each of them that makes that person trustworthy.

Have groups pray together for each other's ability to trust and for their quest to become trustworthy. Have them commit to God their steps toward becoming more trusting and trustworthy.

DEPTHFINDER

UNDERSTANDING THESE KIDS

While their parents probably grew up leaving their doors unlocked, today's junior high students were born into a world in which they couldn't talk to strangers, couldn't go out after dark, and couldn't eat unwrapped candy in their trick or treat baskets. Some of them were abused or neglected as children. Is it any wonder they have trouble trusting other people?

According to a recent survey published in the book *Right From Wrong* by Josh McDowell and Bob Hostetler, 32 percent of churched young people in America say that they usually mistrust people. For students to display the kind of loving trust God desires, they must learn to separate healthy caution toward the outside world from unhealthy mistrust and cynicism toward everything and everyone they come into contact with.

As you prepare and lead this study, pray often for your kids to learn to trust again in the way God desires. No matter what has happened in the lives of your young people, God is able to heal the distrustful spirit so prevalent in this generation.

Who's to Trust?

I TRUST someone when he or she…	**I DISTRUST** someone when he or she…

One way I can become more **TRUSTING** is…

One way I can become more **TRUSTWORTHY** is…

Accept No Substitutes!

How Substitutes for Real Love Can Destroy Your Life

by Trevor Simpson

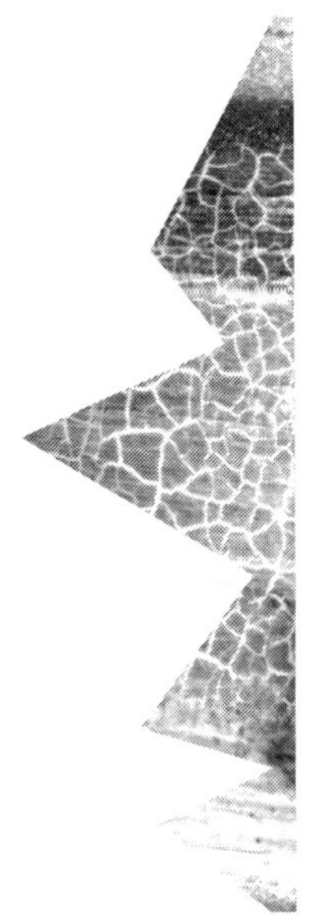

■ Who am I? What am I doing here? What good am I? Where do I go from here? Am I loved? ■ They're questions we all ask but seldom talk about. We're all trying to gain a sense of identity and acceptance in the real world to help us overcome negative emotions like loneliness and despair. Unfortunately, too often we try to find that identity in deceptive substitutes for love rather than in the real thing. ■ Your kids are no exception. Some of them strive to find "love" in school or athletics and other performance-based activities. Others choose drugs, alcohol, or sex to provide an identity. Whatever the tactic, their goal is the same—to convince themselves once and for all that they really are loved. ■ The only problem is that it doesn't work. ■ Use this study to help kids explore ways people get trapped by love's substitutes and to challenge kids to call upon the genuine love of Jesus Christ to give them a true sense of worth and acceptance.

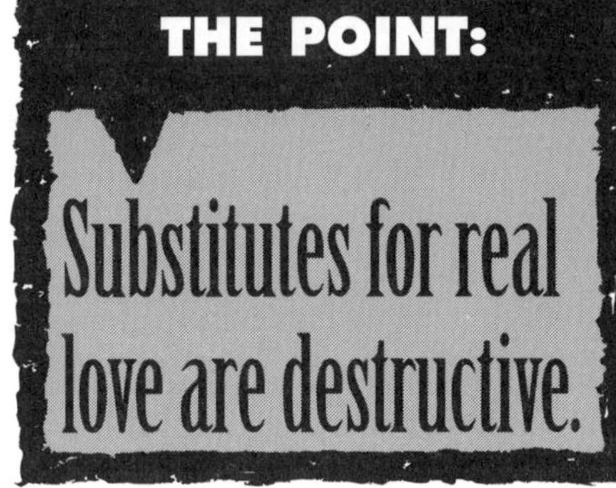

The Study AT A GLANCE

SECTION	MINUTES	WHAT STUDENTS WILL DO	SUPPLIES
Opening Game	15 to 20	VIRUS—Play a game that illustrates how substitutes for love are destructive.	Bible, deck of cards, background music, newsprint, marker
Real-Life Investigation	10 to 15	PERSONAL PROFILES—Read and discuss profiles of real-life individuals who have been fooled by substitutes for love.	"Personal Profiles" handouts (pp. 49-50), "Personal Profiles Discussion Guide" handouts (p. 51), markers, newsprint
Bible Study	15 to 20	BIBLE DISCUSSION—Explore God's love by examining Scripture and discussing what they find.	Bibles, markers, newsprint, tape, "Bible Study" handouts (pp. 52-54)
Personal Experience and Evaluation	5 to 10	TIME WITH JESUS—Reflect on an interaction with Jesus, and identify areas in which they are finding false love.	Bible, "Time With Jesus" dramatic reading (p. 55), paper, pencils

notes:

THE POINT OF "ACCEPT NO SUBSTITUTES!":

Substitutes for real love are destructive.

THE BIBLE CONNECTION

JEREMIAH 2:13	The prophet shares how the Israelites have forsaken God and tried to get their needs met in their own ways.
MATTHEW 5:27-30	Jesus teaches on adultery and explains how we should respond to this sin.
1 CORINTHIANS 6:9-11	Paul explains that wickedness jeopardizes our inheritance of God's kingdom.
1 CORINTHIANS 6:19-20	Paul explains that each individual Christian is also a temple for God.
1 JOHN 4:9-10	John explains that God showed his love for us by sending Jesus to die for our sins.

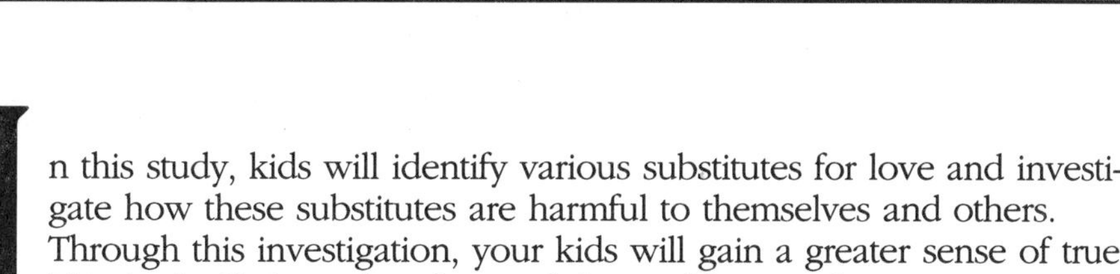

In this study, kids will identify various substitutes for love and investigate how these substitutes are harmful to themselves and others. Through this investigation, your kids will gain a greater sense of true identity in Christ and understand that real love and acceptance are not based on what they do or who they are.

LEADER TIP for The Study

Because this topic can be so powerful and relevant to kids' lives, your group members may be tempted to get caught up in issues and lose sight of the deeper biblical principle found in The Point. Help your kids grasp The Point by guiding them to focus on the biblical investigation and discussing how God's truth connects with reality in their lives.

THE STUDY

OPENING GAME ▼

Virus (15 to 20 minutes)

Gather the group together, and say: **To start off our time together today, we're going to play a game called Virus. The object of the game is really up to you. You can either try to avoid the virus at all costs, or you can decide to play recklessly and try to catch the virus. You see, the virus has some interesting side effects—some are good and some are not so good.**

for Virus

This game will work best if an adult leader is set up to start off as the virus in the first game. To do this, put the ace of spades at the bottom of the deck or remove it altogether so the leader is guaranteed to be the virus.

for Virus

This game will be most effective if several different rooms can be used simultaneously. If this is not possible, consider taking the group outside for this activity. Holding the game in a small room will shorten the game time because the virus will quickly infect everyone.

First, let's examine the good side effects. If you catch the virus, it will give you an abundance of wealth, beauty, and happiness for ten years. You will be able to get away with anything and not get into trouble, and it will solve any problem. The only bad side effect is that when the ten years are up, so are you. The virus will kill you.

The rules of the game are simple. First, you must play within the designated area. Failure to follow this rule will result in instant death and will disqualify you. Second, you must not cheat. If you get the virus, you must become a carrier and try to infect other people. Third, you must always be moving and you may not cover up your elbows. Now, here's how it works.

Each of you will draw a card from the deck, and whoever gets the ace of spades is the initial virus. If you are the virus, or if you become the virus, you must keep it a secret. Once you become the virus, you must try to infect other people. You infect people by quietly, gently, and secretly pinching them on one of their elbows. The game ends after five minutes or when everyone has been infected. We will play this game a couple of times.

Separate one card for each student from the deck. Make sure one card is the ace of spades. Let each student take a card from the stack of cards. Turn out the lights, turn up the music, and let the game begin. Play two or three rounds to give kids a chance to try different tactics or approaches to the game.

When the game is over, gather the students together and discuss these questions:

- **Did you choose to become infected or try to avoid infection? Why?**
- **How is that like or unlike the way you approach real life?**
- **How is this game similar to the situations we face in real life?**
- **Do you think this virus really exists in the world today? Why or why not?**

Say: **The virus in our game was not real, but there is a type of "sickness" in our society that promises exactly what our virus promised, and, like our virus, leads people to death.**

Ask:

- **What do you think that sickness is? Explain.**
- **What are some examples of that sickness that you see in our society? Explain.**

List kids' responses on newsprint. Then have a volunteer read aloud **1 Corinthians 6:9-11, 19-20.** Then say: **All the sinful qualities listed in this passage represent a category of sickness in our society that can be called "substitutes for love." Everyone needs love, but sometimes we don't feel loved or we may be afraid that no one will really love us for who we are. And so we're tempted to turn to a substitute for love to fill the emptiness inside. For example, lots of people use sex as a substitute for love. Or popularity. Or excellence in school. Or even money. These substitutes can make us feel better about life for**

a while, but in the end they'll destroy us. <u>Substitutes for real love are destructive</u>. Let me show you what I mean.

REAL-LIFE INVESTIGATION ▼

Personal Profiles

(10 to 15 minutes)

Form pairs, and give each pair newsprint and a marker. Say: **In a moment, you and your partner will be given a profile of an actual person. Read through the profile, and answer the questions that are provided. Choose one person to write your pair's responses to the questions on the newsprint. As a pair, try to guess the person your profile describes. When we all come back together, I'll ask you to share about your assigned profile and together we'll try to figure out who he really is.**

Give each pair copies of one of the profiles from the "Personal Profiles" handout (pp. 49-50). Also give each pair a copy of the "Personal Profiles Discussion Guide" handout (p. 51). Allow five minutes for kids to discuss and compile their information. Then gather the pairs back together, and have them each highlight the characteristics of their profile with the whole group.

Once all the profiles have been briefly highlighted, have each pair find one other pair that had the other profile. Have foursomes discuss these questions:

- **How are these people like average, everyday people? Unlike?**
- **Which "profile" person are you most like? Explain.**
- **These profiles represent two examples of how people get caught by substitutes for love. What are some other substitutes for love that junior high school students face?**
- **Why do you think we struggle with substitutes for love?**

Have groups guess who their profiles describe. Then share the right answers with the whole group. Say: **Although we may not consider these people to be everyday, average people, it is clear that we could turn out to be just like them. All of us are tempted to use unhealthy substitutes for love, just as they were. <u>Substitutes for real love are destructive.</u> But if we are willing to open up and let God genuinely love us, then we won't be fooled into pursuing unhealthy substitutes for love.**

> **LEADER TIP for Personal Profiles**
>
> The personal profiles are actual people. Each person decided to seek love in different ways and gained his or her identity in different ways.
>
> **Profile 1** This is the story of Hall of Fame baseball player Mickey Mantle. Mantle was one of the greatest baseball players of all time. He played baseball for seventeen years (2,401 games), batted .298, and hit 536 home runs. He was league MVP three times. (Information here and on the "Personal Profiles" handout taken from *The Mick* by Mickey Mantle and Herb Gluck.)
>
> **Profile 2** This is a biography of St. Augustine of Hippo. Augustine was a theologian in the early church and formulated many doctrines that are still taught and practiced today. (Information here and on the "Personal Profiles" handout taken from *Church History in Plain Language* by Bruce Shelley.)

BIBLE STUDY ▼

Bible Discussion

(15 to 20 minutes)

Have kids remain in groups of four, and give each group more newsprint. Write these questions on newsprint and tape the newsprint to the wall so all students can see them:

- What does God want for us?
- How does God help us seek what he wants for our lives?

● Why do you think God tells us that some things are right and others are wrong?

Give groups about five minutes to discuss the three questions. When groups finish, give them each a different section from the "Bible Study" handout (pp. 52-54). Say: **Now let's look at what God teaches about human love and Christlike love and how each affects our lives. Take ten minutes to look up the passage on your handout section and answer the questions provided. Record your answers on the newsprint.**

After ten minutes, say: **Using what you have just learned from the Bible, complete these two sentences within your group:**

● **Foolish substitutes for love give us...**

● **God's true love gives us...**

After each group completes the sentences, have kids rejoin you in one large group. Ask kids to share how they answered the questions and completed the sentences. Then ask:

● **Did your opinion about what God wants for us change as you read your passage? Why or why not?**

● **How would you answer those first three questions now?**

● **Why do you think substitutes for real love are destructive?**

PERSONAL EXPERIENCE AND EVALUATION ▼

To make the "Time With Jesus" dramatic reading more effective, practice reading the story aloud several times before the study. Or if dramatic reading isn't your strength, ask a dramatically gifted volunteer or young person to read it for the class.

Time With Jesus

(5 to 10 minutes)

Turn off the lights. Then say: **When it is completely quiet, I would like all of you to shut your eyes and listen carefully to what I am going to read.**

Read aloud the "Time With Jesus" dramatic reading (p. 55).

When the dramatic reading is over, ask:

● **How does this picture of Jesus match your idea of him?**

● **What is the writer saying about our relationship with Jesus? Explain.**

Read aloud **1 John 4:9-10**. Then say: **God showed his love for us by sending Jesus to die on the cross for our sins—even though we never did anything to deserve it. Because of God's gift of forgiveness, we don't need to perform to be loved and accepted by God. And we don't need substitutes for love because his love is real. Substitutes for real love are destructive, but we have the "real thing" in Christ.**

Have kids close their eyes and then say: **Identify a substitute for love that you need to let go of. Be honest. Jesus is here with you, and he wants to be with you. What substitute for love are you going to rid yourself of today?**

After a few moments, gather the group together in a circle and have them join hands. Close with prayer, asking God to help kids let go of any substitutes for love they have in their lives and accept God's genuine love and acceptance.

Personal Profiles

Photocopy the following profiles so each group gets one.

PERSONAL PROFILE #1

I was born in a small town in Oklahoma. My family was poor, and we never had that much because the communities I lived in were just beginning to recover from economic problems. You could say that my parents were traditional—they had a good marriage.

I grew to be a big and strong young man. I was a football star and a baseball star at my high school. After high school, I played baseball with a minor-league team associated with the New York Yankees. I was doing very well and eventually got called up to try out for the team. I was an outfielder, and during this time the New York Yankees were legendary and had legendary players at virtually every position.

I finally got a chance to play, and I did very well. I played with the Yankees for seventeen years and won the Most Valuable Player Award three times. As great as that sounds, it wasn't always the best. I wasn't able to see my wife and children very often, and I would often feel bored and lonely when we were on the road. Many of my Yankee teammates would go to the bars to find women and get drunk. I would go with them to do the same. I felt like it was a safe thing to do because I knew I wouldn't get caught, and if I did, I would always be able to get out of it.

Over the years, I became a full-fledged alcoholic. I'm not sure why it happened. I guess I felt invincible because of who I was and what I did. Alcohol gave me something that I was lacking. I am sure my alcohol problem took a couple of years off of my baseball career. I know my alcohol problem hurt my wife and my children because they saw me in such pathetic states. As I grew older, I developed cirrhosis of the liver and died early because of alcohol abuse.

PERSONAL PROFILE #2

I was born in North Africa, in a country known today as Algeria. As I grew up, many people around me believed I had superior intelligence—especially my parents. As a result, they provided me with the finest education available. They were good people. My father was a passive, easygoing man who really didn't care much for spiritual things. My mother, however, was a strong Christian, and she expected her children to do what was right and to maintain high moral standards in life.

As I got older, though, I rejected my mother's guidance and drifted away from the lifestyle she wanted me to follow. During the time I was at the university in the North African capital of Carthage, I fell in love with a beautiful woman. We lived together for thirteen years and had a son together—even though we weren't married. During that time, I also indulged in countless sexual encounters with other women. In time, I realized my lifestyle would inevitably lead me to bitterness and despair. And so I began searching for the truth.

At first, I turned to the Bible on my own, but it didn't appeal to me at all. It seemed so crude and barbarous. I found another religion that seemed to explain my inner torment much more clearly, and I began to follow its teachings earnestly. Everything seemed better for a while—until some time later, when I was confronted with the Bible a second time. You see, I loved public speaking, and I had heard of a bishop at a Christian church who was an eloquent speaker. I visited his church to study how he spoke so I could improve my own speaking skills.

This man was teaching from the same Bible that I had labeled crude and barbaric, yet, his words were not only eloquent, but intellectual and concise. For the first time, I understood that I must trust Christ to be my Lord and Savior through his death on the cross.

From that point on, I studied to become a Bible scholar. My schooling and leadership skills had equipped me to become a powerful figure within the church. Eventually I went on to shape many Christian doctrines that are still followed today.

Personal Profiles Discussion Guide

Read the personal profile and then answer the following questions within your group. Write your answers on the newsprint provided.

1. How did this individual strive to find love and acceptance in life?

2. Were his methods for finding love helpful or self-destructive? Explain.

3. What's one lesson you can learn about love based on this person's profile?

BIBLE STUDY

Photocopy this handout so each group can have one.

Jeremiah 2:13 "My people have committed two sins: They have forsaken me, the spring of living water, and have dug their own cisterns, broken cisterns that cannot hold water."

- What had God's people done?

- How do people today most often forsake God?

- How are the cisterns (huge tanks made to hold water) similar to the substitutes for love people go after today?

- What personal "cisterns" are you sometimes tempted to go after?

BIBLE STUDY

Photocopy this handout so each group can have one .

Matthew 5:27-30 "You have heard that it was said, 'Do not commit adultery.' But I tell you that anyone who looks at a woman lustfully has already committed adultery with her in his heart. If your right eye causes you to sin, gouge it out and throw it away. It is better for you to lose one part of your body than for your whole body to be thrown into hell. And if your right hand causes you to sin, cut it off and throw it away. It is better for you to lose one part of your body than for your whole body to go into hell."

- Why did Jesus use such strong language?

- Why don't Christians take these verses literally?

- This passage is talking about sexual lust. What are some other kinds of lust that cause us to rebel against God?

BIBLE STUDY

Photocopy this handout so each group can have one.

I Corinthians 6:19-20 "Do you not know that your body is a temple of the Holy Spirit, who is in you, whom you have received from God? You are not your own; you were bought at a price. Therefore honor God with your body."

- What are temples used for?

- What are some things people can do to worship God with their bodies?

Time With Jesus

Jesus had invited me to spend an hour with him. I was a bit uptight about it, so for days I got ready for my time with him. I wrote down all of these questions I have been struggling with for some time now. What is up with evolution and creation? Why do you let war happen, God? How come most Christians act like my non-Christian friends? Why is there such a thing as zits? Wouldn't it be easier for us if you would yell out of the sky every so often to remind us that there is a God up there, because sometimes I am not so sure.

I spent hours looking through the Bible just in case he would ask me a question. I wanted him to know that I read the Bible, sometimes.

I got a haircut, put on my best outfit, and made Jesus a bracelet as a gift. I didn't want to buy him anything because people always say that handmade gifts are better because they come from the heart.

Suddenly, he walked in the door and sat right in front of me. There he was—God sitting in my midst. I couldn't talk at first. I stuttered and got really sweaty. I felt like he could see right through me.

I immediately fell to my face and started kissing his feet. I wasn't planning on doing that, it just kind of happened. Jesus put his hand on my shoulder and said, "Let's just sit here together."

I didn't know what to say, so I just started babbling incoherently. He probably thought I had been drinking. He said: "Relax! I just like to be here with you and enjoy the scenery from the window. The river and the skyline look beautiful today." I glanced outside, but I barely noticed the scenery. I wanted to jump into my first question. After all, he was only staying for an hour, and I had a ton of questions.

I asked why wars are going on all over the place. He replied, "What does that have to do with enjoying the scenery?"

I was confused and very silent. To break the weirdness of the quiet, I asked another question: "How come being a Christian is difficult? If being a Christian was easier, I'm sure more people would get into heaven."

Jesus said, "Aren't you happy to spend a few minutes with me without having to worry about something you cannot understand?"

More silence. I decided to ask him if he wanted some juice.

He replied: "No, thank you. I would like to spend some quiet time alone with you, though." He went on to say, "I have a question for you. Do you love me?"

I said: "Lord, you know everything. You know that I love you."

Jesus gently scolded, "I liked that when Peter said it, but is it really you?"

"You are not making this meeting very easy, Jesus," I replied.

"You are the one that is making it hard," he replied. "I just like to spend time with you, sharing my presence with you and assuring you of my love. You don't have to entertain me when we are together. Let us just be together."

More silence. "Who do you say that I am?" he asked, nudging my shoulder.

I started rattling, "Well, I'm with the experts, Lord, that say that you are the Creator, Master, Lord of the Universe, Incarnate Word of God, and the Supreme Being from whom greater beings cannot be conceived."

Jesus started laughing and stood up and gave me a huge bearhug.

"You are impossible, but I still love you!" he roared.

Then he left, still laughing. I didn't think it was funny at all. I went out to the window looking for him and feeling confused.

When I got a complete hold on my senses, I realized that I had a bunch of things to do that day.

Then I really missed him.

(adapted from "That Hour With Jesus" by Father Armand Nigro, S.J.)

"This is how God showed his love among us: he sent his one and only Son into the world that we might live through him. This is love: not that we loved God, but that he loved us and sent his Son as an atoning sacrifice for our sins."

why Active and Interactive Learning works with teenagers

Let's Start With the Big Picture

Think back to a major life lesson you've learned.

Got it? Now answer these questions:

- Did you learn your lesson from something you read?
- Did you learn it from something you heard?
- Did you learn it from something you experienced?

If you're like 99 percent of your peers, you answered "yes" only to the third question—you learned your life lesson from something you experienced.

This simple test illustrates the most convincing reason for using active and interactive learning with young people: People learn best through experience. Or to put it even more simply, people learn by doing.

Learning by doing is what active learning is all about. No more sitting quietly in chairs and listening to a speaker expound theories about God—that's passive learning. Active learning gets kids out of their chairs and into the experience of life. With active learning, kids get to *do* what they're studying. They *feel* the effects of the principles you teach. They *learn* by experiencing truth firsthand.

Active learning works because it recognizes three basic learning needs and uses them in concert to enable young people to make discoveries on their own and to find practical life applications for the truths they believe.

So what are these three basic learning needs?

1. Teenagers need action.
2. Teenagers need to think.
3. Teenagers need to talk.

Read on to find out exactly how these needs will be met by using the active and interactive learning techniques in Group's Core Belief Bible Study Series in your youth group.

1. Teenagers Need Action

Aircraft pilots know well the difference between passive and active learning. Their passive learning comes through listening to flight instructors and reading flight-instruction books. Their active learning comes through actually flying an airplane or flight simulator. Books and lectures may be helpful, but pilots really learn to fly by manipulating a plane's controls themselves.

We can help young people learn in a similar way. Though we may engage students passively in some reading and listening to teachers, their understanding and application of God's Word will really take off through simulated and real-life experiences.

Forms of active learning include simulation games; role-plays; service projects; experiments; research projects; group pantomimes; mock trials; construction projects; purposeful games; field trips; and, of course, the most powerful form of active learning—real-life experiences.

We can more fully explain active learning by exploring four of its characteristics:

- **Active learning is an adventure.** Passive learning is almost always predictable. Students sit passively while the teacher or speaker follows a planned outline or script.

In active learning, kids may learn lessons the teacher never envisioned. Because the leader trusts students to help create the learning experience, learners may venture into unforeseen discoveries. And often the teacher learns as much as the students.

- **Active learning is fun and captivating.** What are we communicating when we say, "OK, the fun's over—time to talk about God"? What's the hidden message? That joy is separate from God? And that learning is separate from joy?

What a shame.

Active learning is not joyless. One seventh-grader we interviewed clearly remembered her best Sunday school lesson: "Jesus was the light, and we went into a dark room and shut off the lights. We had a candle, and we learned that Jesus is the light and the dark can't shut off the light." That's active learning. Deena enjoyed the lesson. She had fun. And she learned.

Active learning intrigues people. Whether they find a foot-washing experience captivating or maybe a bit uncomfortable, they learn. And they learn on a level deeper than any work sheet or teacher's lecture could ever reach.

- **Active learning involves everyone.** Here the difference between passive and active learning becomes abundantly clear. It's like the difference between watching a football game on television and actually playing in the game.

The "trust walk" provides a good example of involving everyone in active learning. Half of the group members put on blindfolds; the other half serve as guides. The "blind" people trust the guides to lead them through the building or outdoors. The guides prevent the blind people from falling down stairs or tripping over rocks. Everyone needs to participate to learn the inherent lessons of trust, faith, doubt, fear, confidence, and servanthood. Passive spectators of this experience would learn little, but participants learn a great deal.

- **Active learning is focused through debriefing.** Activity simply for activity's sake doesn't usually result in good learning. Debriefing—evaluating an experience by discussing it in pairs or small groups—helps focus the experience and draw out its meaning. Debriefing helps sort and order the information students gather during the experience. It helps learners relate the recently experienced activity to their lives.

The process of debriefing is best started immediately after an experience. We use a three-step process in debriefing: reflection, interpretation, and application.

Reflection—This first step asks the students, "How did you feel?" Active-learning experiences typically evoke an emotional reaction, so it's appropriate to begin debriefing at that level.

Some people ask, "What do feelings have to do with education?" Feelings have everything to do with education. Think back again to that time in your life when you learned a big lesson. In all likelihood, strong feelings accompanied that lesson. Our emotions tend to cement things into our memories.

When you're debriefing, use open-ended questions to probe feelings. Avoid questions that can be answered with a "yes" or "no." Let your learners know that there are no wrong answers to these "feeling" questions. Everyone's feelings are valid.

Interpretation—The next step in the debriefing process asks, "What does this mean to you? How is this experience like or unlike some other aspect of your life?" Now you're asking people to identify a message or principle from the experience.

You want your learners to discover the message for themselves. So instead of telling students your answers, take the time to ask questions that encourage self-discovery. Use Scripture and discussion in pairs or small groups to explore how the actions and effects of the activity might translate to their lives.

Alert! Some of your people may interpret wonderful messages that you never intended. That's not failure! That's the Holy Spirit at work. God allows us to catch different glimpses of his kingdom even when we all look through the same glass.

Application—The final debriefing step asks, "What will you do about it?" This step moves learning into action. Your young people have shared a common experience. They've discovered a principle. Now they must create something new with what they've just experienced and interpreted. They must integrate the message into their lives.

The application stage of debriefing calls for a decision. Ask your students how they'll change, how they'll grow, what they'll do as a result of your time together.

2. Teenagers Need to Think

Today's students have been trained not to think. They aren't dumber than previous generations. We've simply conditioned them not to use their heads.

You see, we've trained our kids to respond with the simplistic answers they think the teacher wants to hear. Fill-in-the-blank student workbooks and teachers who ask dead-end questions such as "What's the capital of Delaware?" have produced kids and adults who have learned not to think.

And it doesn't just happen in junior high or high school. Our children are schooled very early not to think. Teachers attempt to help kids read with nonsensical fill-in-the-blank drills, word scrambles, and missing-letter puzzles.

Helping teenagers think requires a paradigm shift in how we teach. We need to plan for and set aside time for higher-order thinking and be willing to reduce our time spent on lower-order parroting. Group's Core Belief Bible Study Series is designed to help you do just that.

Thinking classrooms look quite different from traditional classrooms. In most church environments, the teacher does most of the talking and hopes that knowledge will transmit from his or her brain to the students'. In thinking settings, the teacher coaches students to ponder, wonder, imagine, and problem-solve.

3. Teenagers Need to Talk

Everyone knows that the person who learns the most in any class is the teacher. Explaining a concept to someone else is usually more helpful to the explainer than to the listener. So why not let the students do more teaching? That's one of the chief benefits of letting kids do the talking. This process is called interactive learning.

What is interactive learning? Interactive learning occurs when students discuss and work cooperatively in pairs or small groups.

Interactive learning encourages learners to work together. It honors the fact that students can learn from one another, not just from the teacher. Students work together in pairs or small groups to accomplish shared goals. They build together, discuss together, and present together. They teach each other and learn from one another. Success as a group is celebrated. Positive interdependence promotes individual and group learning.

Interactive learning not only helps people learn but also helps learners feel better about themselves and get along better with others. It accomplishes these things more effectively than the independent or competitive methods.

Here's a selection of interactive learning techniques that are used in Group's Core Belief Bible Study Series. With any of these models, leaders may assign students to specific partners or small groups. This will maximize cooperation and learning by preventing all the "rowdies" from linking up. And it will allow for new friendships to form outside of established cliques.

Following any period of partner or small-group work, the leader may reconvene the entire class for large-group processing. During this time the teacher may ask for reports or discoveries from individuals or teams. This technique builds in accountability for the teacherless pairs and small groups.

Pair-Share—With this technique each student turns to a partner and responds to a question or problem from the teacher or leader. Every learner responds. There are no passive observers. The teacher may then ask people to share their partners' responses.

Study Partners—Most curricula and most teachers call for Scripture passages to be read to the whole class by one person. One reads; the others doze.

Why not relinquish some teacher control and let partners read and react with each other? They'll all be involved—and will learn more.

Learning Groups—Students work together in small groups to create a model, design artwork, or study a passage or story; then they discuss what they learned through the experience. Each person in the learning group may be assigned a specific role. Here are some examples:

Reader

Recorder (makes notes of key thoughts expressed during the reading or discussion)

Checker (makes sure everyone understands and agrees with answers arrived at by the group)

Encourager (urges silent members to share their thoughts)

When everyone has a specific responsibility, knows what it is, and contributes to a small group, much is accomplished and much is learned.

Summary Partners—One student reads a paragraph, then the partner summarizes the paragraph or interprets its meaning. Partners alternate roles with each paragraph.

The paraphrasing technique also works well in discussions. Anyone who wishes to share a thought must first paraphrase what the previous person said. This sharpens listening skills and demonstrates the power of feedback communication.

Jigsaw—Each person in a small group examines a different concept, Scripture, or part of an issue. Then each teaches the others in the group. Thus, all members teach, and all must learn the others' discoveries. This technique is called a jigsaw because individuals are responsible to their group for different pieces of the puzzle.

JIGSAW EXAMPLE

Here's an example of a jigsaw.

Assign four-person teams. Have teammates each number off from one to four. Have all the Ones go to one corner of the room, all the Twos to another corner, and so on.

Tell team members they're responsible for learning information in their numbered corners and then for teaching their team members when they return to their original teams.

Give the following assignments to various groups:

Ones: Read Psalm 22. Discuss and list the prophecies made about Jesus.

Twos: Read Isaiah 52:13–53:12. Discuss and list the prophecies made about Jesus.

Threes: Read Matthew 27:1-32. Discuss and list the things that happened to Jesus.

Fours: Read Matthew 27:33-66. Discuss and list the things that happened to Jesus.

After the corner groups meet and discuss, instruct all learners to return to their original teams and report what they've learned. Then have each team determine which prophecies about Jesus were fulfilled in the passages from Matthew.

Call on various individuals in each team to report one or two prophecies that were fulfilled.

You Can Do It Too!

All this information may sound revolutionary to you, but it's really not. God has been using active and interactive learning to teach his people for generations. Just look at Abraham and Isaac, Jacob and Esau, Moses and the Israelites, Ruth and Boaz. And then there's Jesus, who used active learning all the time!

Group's Core Belief Bible Study Series makes it easy for you to use active and interactive learning with your group. The active and interactive elements are automatically built in! Just follow the outlines, and watch as your kids grow through experience and positive interaction with others.

FOR DEEPER STUDY

For more information on incorporating active and interactive learning into your work with teenagers, check out these resources:

- *Why Nobody Learns Much of Anything at Church: And How to Fix It,* by Thom and Joani Schultz (Group Publishing) and
- *Do It! Active Learning in Youth Ministry,* by Thom and Joani Schultz (Group Publishing).

the truth about LOVE

Group Publishing, Inc.
Attention: Core Belief Talk-Back
P.O. Box 481
Loveland, CO 80539
Fax: (970) 669-1994

Please help us continue to provide innovative and useful resources for ministry. After you've led the studies in this volume, take a moment to fill out this evaluation; then mail or fax it to us at the address above. Thanks!

●●●●●●

1. As a whole, this book has been (circle one)

not very helpful								very helpful	
1	2	3	4	5	6	7	8	9	10

2. The best things about this book:

3. How this book could be improved:

4. What I will change because of this book:

5. Would you be interested in field-testing future Core Belief Bible Studies and giving us your feedback? If so, please complete the information below:

Name ______________________________

Street address ______________________________

City ____________________ State __________ Zip __________

Daytime telephone (____) ____________________ Date __________

THANKS!